POETRY LOCUS

VOLUME ONE

By
Yahannan Khan

Copyright © 2025 All rights reserved.

No part of this book may be reproduced, stored in a retrieval system, or transmitted in any form or by any means, electronic, mechanical, photocopying, recording, or otherwise, without the prior written permission of the copyright owner, except for brief quotations used in reviews or scholarly works.

ISBN: 9798893974881
Printed in the United States of America

Dedication

To all my wonderful linguistics teachers, your wisdom and passion for teaching have been a guiding light on poetic paths.

To the awesome folk over at St. Peter's Erindale, who each and all afforded effort to make a milestone life event magical for a tropical soul in temperate lands.
Loved ones endeared, siblings, friends... DABs and ChERuBs!

Above all, to the One, above all.

Thank you

Acknowledgments

No journey is ever undertaken alone, and this work stands as a testament to the many hands, hearts, and minds that have shaped my path.

To my teachers throughout the years, especially those who nurtured my love for language, literature, and critical thought in English Language, English Literature, and The General Paper at Jamaica College, your guidance laid the foundation for my voice as a writer. I am grateful for the lessons, the challenges, and the inspiration that continue to resonate in my work. To the publishing team, who debugged the so many jitters, to make this book a reality!

To my late parents, whose unwavering belief in me gave every reason to dream, strive, and become. Your love and sacrifices remain the compass that guides me forward.

To my friends, the kindred spirits who have walked beside me, sharing in both the trials and triumphs, your presence has made every step of the journey worthwhile.

And above all, to the One alone, without whom life, let alone poetry, would not be possible.

With deepest gratitude,

Yahannan Khan

Table of content

COMFORT	7
DAISIES	9
EMBLEM	10
FALLING	12
GROWING	14
HEARKEN	15
INK LINES	17
LAMBLION	18
MIRRORS	19
NEW	21
OPINED EYES	22
PELE PLETHORA	24
QUERY CITY	26
RIB	27
SANDY WORDS	29
TENSE BINDS	30
UNCURTAIN	31
WHETHER	32
YAY YE! HA DADLE	33
WITHIN WITHOUT	35
UP ACHE	38
TIS THE URN	40
THE THREE PYRE EIGHTS	41
THE VULCANE OH!	43
THE GREY LION	44
THE PRE-CIOUS	45
THE SEER	46
STORAGE	48
SNOWFLAKE RIVER	50
SALAMANDER	51
THE SOWER	52
RAYING	54
PICO	56
OCEAN HOME	59
OBJECTION	61

NE CATION	62
LOVELAND	63
LETTER	64
LE MON DROPS	66
LANDED OARS	68
IMPORTANT	70
HEROSE	72
HEART STEADY	77
EPIC UR	79
DAYS OF YEARS, IN TIME OF SEASON	81
CAST OF SHADOWS	83
C- OH FRESH A LEAF?!	85
GOD AND THE DEVIL	89
BLUE HANDS	91
BELIEF WITHIN, SELF WITHOUT	92
BEGINNINGS	94
AVA DENSE	95
ALL GOOD THINGS	97
ABYSMAL ARTISAN	98
ABOVE CHAOS	99
4 ME	100

COMFORT

Then with the plight of troubled mind
The Seeker seeks if so to find a place
Where comfort living dwells amidst the spin of cares

The Seeker sought both high and low the places
Where few others go
The matter so to truly know but scarcely was one there

The comfort sought not sold nor bought
The one that soothes the bittern thought
The needed one of much retort
For such the seeker toiled

Inquiring here and trying there
The seeker sought most everywhere
At last to finally declare
The search rewards a spoil

So joyfully the seeker gleed
With great triumphant jubilee
I found I found how good it be
This search that I decreed

For comfort lies not on the shelf
Nor in regard of any self
At last alas I clearly see
That comforter is thrice-fold me!

So on and on fore always seek
In times of strength
At times when weak
And keep the cherry shaded cheek
Alight with joy always

For now I clearly see my friend
By proof at once and yet again
The comforts of a seeking trend
Delights a heart at play.

SRB. 14.2025

DAISIES

Poof goes the proof
Of past things gone

In the pace of the quickened race

Papered chases of wilderness' storms
All offshoots of a collective norm!

With diverse strains
Of ledgered chains
Of events
Blocked in
Distant supply chains break lines
Where things begin

Memories of the just now past,
With bearings now lost
Benches
Bearing marks of a forward cost

All these
Rinks form brinks of the links
Across the plain…

Houses on prairies of life's daisy chain

SRB 01.3.2025

EMBLEM

What then begets a stir of Rhymes
So metered on the changeless times
In face of tales of battles won?

Who knows the ends
Of things begun!

Beginning holds it mystery
While wars betell the history
Of men amidst the troubled plains
Prepared to win at hungered games

At distanced dash are honored names
Dark peerless clouds of gloried fame
The best of men no beast can calm
While nature screams of life's embalm

What first became?
What followed next?
What Holy Spirit first was vexed?
What warriors begot their kings?
What circle doth enclose the rings?

Effects as cause must jointly dwell
If time must have a vibrant swell...
Can cause of other nature come?

What then would multiply the sum?

Wherefore can man remove a scar
To wash these blooded tales of war?
From eyes that nature granted him
To see the truth that lies within?

Wordless thoughts of thoughtless words!

Give ear to men that truth be heard
Thou maker of perfected forms
That of the fixed objects cast
Man may become his best at last

Still...
Of all that is within us clean
We judge
Between base and supreme.
While...
Still holding half the perfect whole
The tale of truth remains untold

Too fast for cares
So onward yet
Hold fast the fill
The rest
Forget!

SRB. 9.2.2025

FALLING

Thoughts of childhood dreams
From yonder
Falling
With star stunned holds of choices ever made
Gripped of unknown fears from fore ward
Calling
Broken peace
Of muffled rounds
Pulsating
Mystic sounds.

Hypostasis
Of
The timely sound
Of
Aquarius grounds
Of
All perfected round
Of

All as one!

At last of sea
Behold we sand!
All makers
Of the ways
Of life's command

In these we hold
To faith as told
From which again
As so we came
That seen as true
Some misconstrue!

When nature
Calls
Our name!

SRB 14.2.2025

GROWING

Know that all within resides
Believe the path with every stride
Check the way the will commands
Give the take at able hands
Chasen every scornful urge
Task the soul itself to purge
Hold the gains
Negate the loss
Yes thine way becomes at last
Make beginnings new at ends

See the light at orbits end?

These small steps I promise you
Serve to make new dreams come true.

SRB 26.02.2025

HEARKEN

Though through forms untold
Within the ear quickened
Soaring, searing seeing comes
The dirth of darts delight
Where spirits pace peace apart
Akin of all ransomed wroth

Joyful jealous rupt
Untangle natures rope

That forms bare, rupture

Each then untold now caves an end
Of spirits epic cure
This way the hearken
Makes its floor,
Be certain, sure secure.

He moves resolved in coming through
The calm of patient poise
Bidding consort of all that emanate,
As fate infers
Without waste, nor doubling haste, the prize, a taste...

No loss of time,
All pressed for pace
No forms without,
Through nature's ear gawking caws
Erupt the clear
Hearken flight,
Of celestial air.

SRB. 12.2024

INK LINES

Is it not with a stray of a distracted glance

That we stare unaware of inclined optic halls

Glances ignored of bored ranks and scores that lend a traction

To this

Or that?

All while holding firm inter-spacial worms that unearth hints and tones

Unanswered phones that might ring

Or they might not?

Stylized wills and wonts mark patterns on fronts where we're not

Awake to so many entangled lines that link, tendered stakes

Streaming rakes

Or brooms

Scales

Or spiralled curves,

Polkadot

Spangles,

Crossing angles

More there is

Between the mind

And its inked lines

SRB 28.1.2025

LAMBLION

Leaps of springy green
Awake with air and flavoured field
So sprang the lamb in full of its day
Amidst still wild early flowers
Late in May

Loudless paws play the clayed course
High vibrant waves all cloud a shield
Apace amidst all hollowed forrows of grassy sway
The now greyed King awaits the hour
With eyes on the prey

Together then at what surely is the last of pleasures
Beauty reasons with grace of joys and leaps of springs
Power seasons the taste of ploys and heaps of things
So bleats the growl!

Applause of every fowl.

SRB 7.2.2025

MIRRORS

As fore thought things
Pre-vent the fall
As mirrors don their sheen
While image hails
The thing that is
While that before is seen

So does the dark
Break forth a ray
So forms the answered spark
So does the joy begets a day
So nests the looming lark

To see that when
The day brings true
It's wonders of delight
Demands it bidding each and all
To set the lines aright

For whom amongst
Does favor not
The savor of the end
Harmonious putting forth of self
Desires so to pen

That when at last the feather flop
When times experienced give
The melodies we make at heart
Become the lives we live

SRB. 2.2025

NEW

To stand together though apart
Entangled highs and lows untold
To each inclined to grasp the hold
Triumphant shields from trepid dart

At last at one,
Above the cold
The new becomes
As time unfold

We dare what comes that stand the fall
To see the beauty of the all
We   perish not
yea rather thrive
Of each, by other we survive

See hold this fast and see it clear
That way beyond
Thee changing year
The stands and band
That knot our ties
Both joy and madness
Multiply.

Happy New Year!!!
SB 1.1.2025

OPINED EYES

I wonder often at the sense
In man the number five
The small cast set amidst a man
Awares of most alive

That sounds the fragrance of the rose
That grants the stomach wrench
That bids the heart lest we forget
The rue of every stench

They stir the minds of some without
They scale the music's note
The take the will to highs and lows
Upon the buoyant float

They warn of heat
They call on cold
They gauge the comfort scale
The whisper to dependent hearts
Of dolphins shark or whale

Without them what becomes of sip
Or labour at a meal?
And with the other spoken next

Give end to served appeal

There still remains but one supreme
On which we most depend
This one alone doth hold the dream
This one doth light the pen

But take care not to go as far
That lone on these depend
Because the master of them all
Determines in the end

When sorted sound
And knowing feel
With scented taste
And sight
Together join to tell the tale...
- Of things that are aright

SRB. 12.2025

PELE PLETHORA

We dwell
Amidst cosmic commands becoming
Things brought about of summing
Logus

Freely willed of the self in focus
That sings the songs of soul
Song of songs of beauty's behold

Fiery frosted
Forms of wilderness' storm
The all embracing norm

With these are the trees beyond sight
Seeds of future delight
Dreams of the eternal light
Flown free of natures night!

Few eyes withhold
The spring
That with it bring
Bewildered plethora
Faun and flora
Casts of the stream that make all clean
Of handled dream

Greater numbers swell
Their tales to tell
With fauna and flora
The Pele Plethora.

SRB. 19.1.2025

QUERY CITY

The things we learned are lessons passed
What things we work are done
All high achievements mark our lines
Still there remains just one

That man may see before their rest
While there's still a chance to grow
That in his form as so be set
Remain that still to know

All answers at the earth's request...
All ways and wayward woe not yet
The colours are the unmade best
Of noble earth with bosom set!

RIB

Bear no despair for things that I may never truly grasp
Fear not the smear while vapor seals these hands that we have clasped
Cheer not the tear the troubles cause to gather 'neath the lids
Swear not to share that life holds all things fast because I live

Just know that there are things without that span the all that is
Remember that all choice is truth as sure as now I live
Consider this that as before in this same worthwhile life
Belief and faith propelled us while we took it all in stride

Do hold it fair when it appears that all around oppose
Do trust the faith that flows within the pair each only knows
Then celebrate the only truth that loving pairs know true
That we have sworn to always and forever see it through

Oh sure the thunders shake the ground
Oh sure the stormy rain
Yet still recall beneath these lids
The vow that holds the rain
And channels through most turbid tides
True guide to later give
The beacon lighthouse
That becomes
That purpose of the rib.

SRB. 12.1. 2025

SANDY WORDS

Ten times a hundred castings forth with numbers more yet still
Are all the words that frame the fort of coloured coats to fill

Each one a silver clouded line of measures modes and ways
That gives to each encumbered mind of treasured length of days

Strong hold for every shooting star that owns the steadied dream
The opus of prospective rest that guide the sanded stream

So that together Sandy Words immersed and washed ashore
Will bring delights to faithful hearts awake to dream no more

Tis thought who watered desert ways to sea the tempered sand
Tis sand that sifts the bevelled rounds of things as they began
Tis rounds that tell the natures tell of things that seem afar
Tis natures tell that brings to life this wish upon this star.

SRB. 04.02.2025

TENSE BINDS

Past events
Present
Future ends

The Imperfect
Continuous present
Perfect past trends

Foreword contents
Express conclusions
Indexed

SRB. 12.2.2025

UNCURTAIN

Sure as the sun a new way brings
Forth of its promise before it's light
Promises tomorrow
Leaves off seeds of starry glittered flight
The thing that is
Becomes its own by rays and waves and base resound
When seeds asleep break out to peep into soils
Proclaiming the life the earth exhales
All finite travails of thingless tails

Who can but love the beauty told
Of these the greatest simple things
The light taking its flight on fluttered wings
Of honeyed stings
Celestial rings sing orbits or constant changing things
With these bring measures of joy to be told
The tales of soaring joys unfold

SRB 15.1.2025
Island Home.

WHETHER

Clearly seen as not yet
Being before
Droplets
Clouds afloat
On unbroken numbered hands
Cupping care
Bring cool
Upon such treasured winds
That it should fall
As it does
And waters mist
As waters must

SRB. 8.2.2025

YAY YE! HA DADLE

Marvelous it is the window
To the eyes of the aged
To see a man as but a tree

First thought then seed

Through growth to wooded arms
To sway with winds
To tug at roots
To bow and bend
And hail the Sun
Taste of waters
Sift it's soil.

And tell in such singularity of gain
The beauty made of it all
Vibrant, colors, sweet and tang
Scented, fragrant, woven hand

To like the tree that once a thought
Remain a static memory wrought!

So too,
Yes we
Here now to bring
Tomorrow

Off the one same thing.

That each perceives
As mind
so gives
Beyond that end
Again to live

In it
Not there
Aren't we all?
Behind the veil
Ahead the fall?

So bluntly hands do cast the change
So everything becomes arranged.

And so....
It evolves.

WITHIN WITHOUT

We perceive without
All who have fallen
From life's options
To its choices

We look intently
While the greater is
Made sacrifice for its meagre extensions

Accepting at face
That these effects need
Be at end of ones rekindle
Resounding at source the one truth

The answer lies with each
And this a law universal
That which we perceive
Is only so
By its truths echo within

There is no man
Nor beast that sees
A thing unknown and rests

That which we believe
Dwells outward,

As it does within

So what then
Do we look?
Do we now see
these lines drawn through?

From what is
In us within
To that which has effect
In others
Without

Do we come to see
That we, also
Have the greatness
Sacrificed
For that held value on display.

Do we see in us
What?
Those without do see
While that within them
Bears sharp the focus

There was one who called it a principle
The reversibility of the light
In one phrase it was taught thus

It is a principle, the reversibility of light
You can see me,
Because I can see you.

But what is law, that it should force a bind
It cares not that one obeys
Rather is shouts a wisdom as overflowing
The streets and by ways
Saying hear
Oh children of the Admah!
Hear me
Ones or the sphere of man!

Thine answer lies
Not
In the other
Man,
Know thy self.

Still what is law to force its bind?
And what is the gain of this thing,
Wisdom?
History will unite us
With wisdom
And our glory with a great mind.

SRB11.2024

UP ACHE

It first appeared clear as the whistle
Sharp bright spectacles of the light
A freely flowing disencumber
Of crisp discern

Elegance of delight
Shape curtains crystal clear
The purest of the freshest air
Sweet subtle perm

From whence it rippled
Folded trickled cascades
Become drapes of the perm
Lingering resound
Compounds of dramatic fills

Glancing flows
Beauty still….until
These next fold themselves
Subtle freshness now casting bold

Chills of freshness
Now as fold give bellowed cold
Emboldened perms thus appear
Shadows
Light patterned drapes

De - Clearing
The Up- Ache

SRB. 29.1.2025

TIS THE URN

Behold the tap
With steady stable stir
Affixed apace
With vibrance still

See now it's curl
That stir of turn
That thing that does
Retain its churn

Still thence it wobbles
Stillness denied
To so part from
The questioned gaze
Of Stillness questioned

Then after churn
What pace it burns
A wobbled perm
That is the urn.

SRB 12.2024.

THE THREE PYRE EIGHTS

We know them not
A few
Of us
We know them
Not with care

We know we know
Then
Not to fear
For now
I list them here.

The first be named
As- Pire

By whom the heights acclaim
And with this be
Pers-Pire
The lines doth this retain
Who can forget
Ins- Pire
The loot is void without!

These three together
All with one
Wroth deeds
Both high and stout!

Together, Can.

THE VULCANE OH!

Above
Cool cascades stream
Lost at once
To fervent folds

Complete
In all yonds
Decrees

Flowering aright

Conceived of depths
Unknown
To heights
Stemming flows

Nature's desert
Natural still
Now cast forth
Commanding spirits

Take flight

SRB 12.2024

THE GREY LION

Good it seems
The raspy rims
That rhythm pens
Entangled trims
Motive to stoke

Who then dost sway
The chorused trance
That holds all
Circled in the dance?

The natures best
For cycles vest
The faunas field
To ends revealed

So when
In time
The test appears
We do ascend
The karmosphere.

Best.

SRB092024

THE PRE-CIOUS

Then, shaking
The sword evolved a spear
By which was made separate
Of science
The 'S'
Yet Cience stood,
Still!

In time
Expanding expanse
Was Cience , now CIOUS
What marvel
This is, as so to call
Upon all that once fore was

To find in this
Pre - Cious science
The life that lay
Before?!!!!

PRECIOUS......
SRB01.10.2024

THE SEER

The seeing one
Rests above the heights of the way
Deeming the rightward streaming of ascending all
Things rightly so to call

The one that sees
Speaks of the eyes that magnetize
Flows of things flown
Mysteries of things still
Yet unknown

Fruited formalities of grounds ploughed through
No delay in paying all due
To this and that thing holding true...
Words of the way of crossings at the stay
The coming of day

Yields of things,
True in- formation
Ascents of the sifts of handless creation
Feed the seed of determined need
A stationed stall
From which to wade the true grade of all...

Things!?

Substance of the forms true nature brings
Feed eyes of eyes well within set
Things neigh worthy to forget
Things firmly set

The seer cast upon the stake
Forms of words all makings make
The hearing, ears quake at flawless dues
Things, misconstrued?

Still at last this fearsome casting forth
Gives
That we endure, sure to live
Lives built on casts of seer's tell
In formation henceforth
We dwell...

SRB. 18.1.2025

STORAGE

Passive silos
Towered, aged things brought forth
Things such as these
Words withhold
Tempered beams brave
Once vibrant rage
Fore casting blocks
Made cold

Momentous
Majestic silent stills
Tales of promise
Futures will
Calming

Solemn cares
Assurance blessed
By treasured chest

That when the due
So circled
Comes with agles shaped on chance
Untroubled mind
Recount the sums
For feet now freed
To dance

SRB. 10.02.2025

SNOWFLAKE RIVER

Snowflakes gather more yet
Still where
Nature's streamings flow
Ebbs of looming oxen
Heads bowed to name
Concaved pools carved, curved
Of resilient ground
From skittled silty loamy shifts
The currents flake on still
Motionless captives
Ripples without flow...

Each form a rapture
Of ruptured harmony
Apace with the haste of streams aflow
Captured on the eyes' catch
To relish next
Glimpse of glimmering sways of a time long past
Together falling
Captive, stalling
Flakes where nature streams.

SRB. 3.2025

SALAMANDER

Do eyes not pierce flaming stills of not long vibrant pens?
Filled with tomorrow's lasting inks of things men think to be
Inspired by the fired light of things all hold as right.
For which men fight

Men inspired by the flame go lighting ways of endless days
Glory , olden golden days where hearts at will have sway
Reports of rising up to play, why wait a day?

The heart's decree defends in time the suspense of holden bars
Craving the star that lights beyond a hill, or higher still.

Flame to flame the gentle stream became itself the how!
The ploughers plough on hills.
Still the substance of men, moving soul's heart command nature stand
Bringing again to pass through latent cast a guiding hand.
The one command

The rest is a patient test or faith!
While here the others wait.

SRB. 14.1.2025

THE SOWER

At once the girded sower cast
The seeds that root the forrow
Alone he sees the fruited fields
Alone he sees tomorrow

High waves to picnicked pleasant folks
He girds his wit yet tighter still
While beams of grimaced pleasant smiles
Sun shades escarping rolling hills

Reaching in, reaching out
Sprinkles of future hope, dashed!

Delighted fauna peep and chirp to say
Oh bless the way, he walks along paths grey
With green unseen.

Pecking peckers peck the decks of grassy folds
Nature's hold, grasped in...let go...dashed!

A glance beyond to see the winds of clouds
The trees aloud...grant shade
Soon efforts made
Increase the shade of suated earth

He holds the girth to give a final yield
Grasping in...reaches out...dashed!

Still time to find a moments rest
To bare the chest of treasures as the wind becomes
The wave that brings the life to dashes of dreams
Seeds soon green, lone tomorrows
Full of fruited fields.

SRB 7.2025

RAYING

Does it seem at most a time to be
This same?
The way nature falls
To make a name
Of
The little things
That usher into pass
Things thought...

To reign at last?

Just quiet silence
Rippling into flow
In face
Of questions answered " I don't know!"
Till last a thing
Weighs on the dense below
As all seeds
Grow

That now
At aged end one places pen
To seal
Thoughts that ripple
Once again
Unseeded thought
Now bears the seeded grass
All thoughts becoming
Cast

Does it not seem....

SRB 14.2.2025

PICO

The weighted bulk of all that is
Possible?
Where,
In it lies the stir?
Of this all needs become.

While having all what need remain?
So that
Becoming it is, and does become!

The matter rests!

Yet still
Becoming
Finding places
Of spaces
Still unknown.

Silent stirs touch
On levers
making
Silent moves to shape the sounds
Massive
Compound

Weights of measures of all
Matters heard
With resound, without answer.

Perfection within,
The bulk without
The answers
Still...
To come.

Express
Expanse latent hold
Keys of finer things!
Single
Sulks of bulk give way
The finer sway
At last a day came
When the bulk of these matter!
And so scatter

Off to be what is
To see...to you: to me

Fine allies of ways
Set free...
No more to be!
A massive bulk of all that is.

Thus vex the flows
Of every stream,
Each creed each team
Build a hope of yonder
Dream on matter's bulk of all fair things
With harpened strings,
Beauty's bulk at the end,
At last.

Pico bulk of all
Does fall.

SRB. 11.1.2025

OCEAN HOME

Desert waters aged, since once ago
Timid
Thighs shiver at the whither of returns'
First reveal
So real
This feel of familiar winds
Unscented
Fragrance above tides now adrift
Sweet fragrant whiff

Next
The wrangle of entangled ends
Left free
Coming back,
There's almost a slap of gentle ends at face and knees

Gentle face
Taps that arouse
Clenching knuckles as knees buckle

In awe of how it's still raw!
All the things we saw...
The knuckles thaw

Then at once a flushing
Thrills that shake features of a face

Out of place

For after this,
Memories of a while ago
Grace reflective faces at sway

With splashes and sprays.
Jerkings of spontaneous smile

At last
With ears forever opened
To past things once shown
Again and as always

No place like home!...

SRB 27.1.2025

OBJECTION

From The Stillness
Through the way of becoming
Thus.
Through prudence,
Guiding,
Guarded,
Becomes.

Away!...
With reasons...

At Oneness
With Peace

SRB. 12.2024

NE CATION

What pray
Be that
Prey

Catapult!
Soaring object
Doing as they
Only do
To its T!

Solitary
Is the nature of the soul
Delights perfected
Of tender bewilderment

They together
Express are.
Common

SRB. 12.2024.

LOVELAND

With eager ear's expecting arms
I waited to be told
By voyagers who course the seas
Those fearless, strong and bold

I waited as the cast approached
The watery shallowed shore
Cascaded spiral spirit surge
At last retained no more

Finding such place as catch a wave
I waited , patient still
Till all the cast had steadied stand
And all the dues were filled

Then not to spare a moment's haste
Then not to earn a sore
The cast began the spin their tales
Of yonder distant shores

Expecting ears with outstretched hands
Received at hearts demand
The seeded fruit adventure yields
To ones who love the land.

SRB. 1.2025!

LETTER

Yes today has gone a way that tomorrow may tell of
Bundles in edges and folds of each construed spell of
Cheer sent to be meant to share, to be made clear of
Doubts about trust now repaired
Through memories endeared.

The convenience of contrived canvas gives gracious space to
Convened pristine stanzas via spacious place too...

Colours red, black and blue, record the crossings through thought
Fermentation of affirmed mentation's shared,
With one who cared,
To spare parts of entangled hearts

Each stroke, each line its salted time
Full flavours of oneness savoured
Now stretched hue laces
Spanning spaces measured in time.
Measures sublime.

Joining these together to make
Known things known
Colours and stroke stoke trust where faith has grown
Flights of passions flown.

These unbound streams all freedoms set
When worlds begin to let!

SRB. 20.1.2025

LE MON DROPS

Much task assigned to self as truth
And oh how long the seeker roots
At depths below the prime of youth
To find the quanta of reboot...

Much talk be said or soul and sins
And where all ends and each begins
Alignment or the source within
That fix each paddle to its pin

Much merchandizing worth in self
Unnumbered books atop the shelf
The touted value built in stealth
Procures of basic path to wealth

Many doors closed
To eyes unseen
The prize opposed
The foe unseen
The chew of fat
The want of lean
And all that is
Therein between

That tasking
Long

In soul

And sin

Alignment

Fix

The Paddle

Pin

The stealth

Of wealth

Doors

Eyes unseen

Prize

Lean

And All

Therein between

SRB. 12.2024

LANDED OARS

Aye aye at last
Sternly brought about
Barnacled boardings of lasting holds
Bring halts to sure
Cold ending waters

Feelings of wanton
Gifted grants knot notted wants
Ageless wearied plays
Hand beholden days!

Perfections of an axis
Carved of whole lives'
Practice
Wrapped seeds embrace
Last callings to grace

Whole ways wide
Hitting
Plane's target wood
Coats that guide
Nearer souls that should
Have it all aright
Beacons of its own light
Perfected aright...

Still who can dare?
What powers bare?
What thoughts compare?
The spark of things
Undone?
Unknown- Unflung?

The Spring not Sprung
Vanity, vanity
Vexatious sore
A voyagers vaults
Of Landed Oar

SRB. 24.1.2025

IMPORTANT

Recounting famous battles
Only a few my own
Appears the becoming,
Beckoning truth.

Not opposed are we
Them versus me?
But, on the very contrary,
Finding we, and me!

Invariably,
Found I
within
The settled dust of tumult
On this side, we
On the other...me!

We, with me?!!!

Causes subside pairs changing
Context, vare as changes serve
As channels of Peace, the rages of war.

Is it too natural?
That which cannot

Retain.

Then, and now,

Yet over again

Must we not unearth...

That we.....in me?

And so....we proceed!

HEROSE

A stranger asked me twice, not once
The measure of the man
Who guides the steady outcome fast
Of where he takes a hand
Who relish all the time well spent
On each and every care
And what the measure speaks about
The things that he hold dear

A friend once bid me think about
The ends that do avail
Of lifetime efforts spent amidst
The beating of the sail
Of focussed steadied steering wheels
On rudders bonded fast
And eyes kept on the future path
Ignoring things that past

A student showed me their discourse
On matters manly made
On how to struggle past the angst
Of making every grade
On rolling with the puches thrown
Of floating with their tide
And braving all that come and go

Stand tall and not to hide

A younger soul inquiring asked
About the futures hold
For men who hardly light the eyes
Men worth their weight in gold
Of worlds and measure made now dust
Beneath the streams reclines
And what to make of all that comes
Of these interesting times

I thought of how to answer
Each their questioning intent
And took a moment to reflect
On hearty random rends
On direst truth in ernest eyes
True cares about life's path
And what the balance ought to be
So not to wroth a wrath

Then something silent whispered in
The ear no eyes can see
YiQh'ra : Qha'ra, the maker wills
All things that ought to be
For when a time and need command
Him worthy of the climb
The workman hears the tutors call
Each one within his time

So measure not what thing now is
Except the rule be true
And while the tally so awaits
Be firm in what to do
For time flows that way then the next
All efforts to distill
At last it is the Ernest seed
That thence refills the till

Of measured man
Of futures hold
Of past things have no tell
For sure as night follows the day
So things that work do well
The ocean bids us watch for sure
As nature's path it tells
Expect the certain concave pull
Of every convexed swell

All measure is of method
All methods good as gold
The treasured secrets lie now hid
In things that can't be told
And each decides the chosen path
Not cowardly nor brave
But as the measure so allows
But as the the way is paved

Hold only these I said at last
To stranger, friend and youth
Stand wisely strong as crest doth rise
While always holding truth
That surely as today does surge
There will arrive a crest
And lifes true measure falls to one
Who truly gives their best
This one great truth no one denies
Who's ever bid to try
And any one who says not so
May well tell you a lie

Much worry is as chewing gum
When food the stomach yearns
The fuel in your chest will yield
The measure of the burn
Stand fast with patient wisdom then
With timing as the friend
And with these tools you nearly always
Brave the bitter end

So toss the weight of measure,then
Of ones who never try
And hold thy burdens in until
The waves belie the cry
The crown is noisome just because
All numbers must so shout

So stand the ground and hold the staff
And know what it's about

These words came through I know not what
The channels that they came
Reflecting on what words I spoke I'd say them all again
For in the final story
In legends cast in lands
The wise and patient yardstick holds the measure of the man.

SRB 5.2025

HEART STEADY

Who then be thou
Within thine stead
Who drive
The feeble to the dread
Of men
Holden past the time of swell
Now so to serve...
What just deserve?

The plight goes on
Aware yet still
No match
For mettled
Rupted will...

Faces places
Smiles with tongue
To slide away
The slanted rung
Rising
Steps made clear of dust
Flaming thoughts
Of rustless rust
Rustic stance
Euphoric sway

A new day
The granted way
Becomes
The path less sung
Spoiled
Soil of battles won
That once begun
Away have spun!

SRB. 11.2026

EPIC UR

Thee opposed to right,
Left as heart so placed
In one so to move
The pulse of circles secret
Mental magistic moves
Life.

That turns blushes glow
Alive with flows
Of streams of living ways
A task each day

While seeming,
Still to stray!
By ways to know
Afar to go
Two feet ten toes
The paddle rows
The epic goes on

To these extremes
Where
Lay visions dream of life
Beyond shapes set
Tears blood and sweat
Now to fore get

The things that must
Rather be...

With prints in desert dust
And with all promise thus
Came substance of trust
Mustered visions of things unseen
Of thoughts held supreme
These empower desert's dream

This epic new is old we know
We share and grow
The seeds that we procure
Of epic Ur.

SRB. 12.2025.

DAYS OF YEARS, IN TIME OF SEASON.

From subtle seeds
Days so break forth
The dawn of noonday Sun
Through courses
Set the noon does pass
The dusk at once begun

Then see
Full, fruit await the time.
Of turning of the Sun
Of shadow
Comes the subtle seed
Again to what was done

For what is day
If not the seed
Of years of seasons lain
With Spring it's dawn
And Summer's noon
It's Autumn fills the Plain

So then doth winter
Bring it's rest
All heat of spring to stay
And this year's night
As that days night
Do cycles in this way.

The All, is fruitful.
Extensions of Comprehensions.

SRB04SEPT2024.

CAST OF SHADOWS

Wherefore does light
Cast forth a beam
Where does the shadow dwell

The light that holds
Of all things true
It's nature so to tell

And when the light
It's object meets
Where then begets it splatter

And of what
Gins Its hidden parts
In former things or latter?

Does then the shadow
Block the path
Of all revealing light

Or does the shadow tell
A tale Of how
Things are aright?

Could not the all
Revealing light

Be telling us from far

That in it's wake
A shadow tells
Us truths of what we are?

For whom is there
That sees a light
Save that it be aspew

So then must we
See shadows still
As what we are as true.

We then from darkness
All each hail
We are its soul and seed

And of these lines
The light doth tell
At every lumens deed.

C- OH FRESH A LEAF?!

Enough is there not in the mystery of the Sun
The life as is just
New days as begun

The life in the air that expresses all forms
The stir of the thickets
The charge at the thorn?

The buzz that terrestrial
Feeds growth
Strong and tall

The waves the derive
Animating us all

The churn and the tingle
The bows and the beads
The herb that without care
Makes good of its seeds

There's enough of a mystery
In just being here!
The kindness of squirrels
That stop then and there

To shiver it's flashes

Of sheer pure delight
The flora and fuana that make it seem right

There's enough of a reason
Is there not as it stands
To gaze at the heavens
The cosmos commands

And know that within us are all things without
And by us and through us they all
Come about

There is enough buoyancy
Just as things are
To know we are one
With all things near and far

The natural truth that
Are made heard and seen
These all are compacted
In our human being!

Still sometimes distracted
We often forget
Our place in the order
Of how things are set

At length so distracted
We look for the gain

Past all pure perfection
That's still just the same

And freely we bonded
Detach and discard
Untangle our sense
Of this cosmic reward

Through snarling and howling
The beauty to cease
We trade in for magic
The thrill of the beast

So surely as cosmos the charge at the point
Increases the senses to densest delight
Commanding the cosmos to make of our will
A compacted conversion
Of spaces we fill

The beauty by birthright
We harvest at once
The nature allowing
It's kings to its dance

The sphere now one formed
Can naught be undone
The form of it casted
No freedom to run

Now fonder we Ponder the beauty once mine
How much we see clearly that each is divine
With longings resolve
And in face of our truth

We then must confirm to the thing we compute!
Now left is the feeling of how to contain
The loss of a memory
Whose music remain

Our pearl as a sphere has our object become
And why should we then live with things left undone?
Of all these our choices what options remain?

We can't very well just go do it again?
And having our pearl
Made of things of our hands
We now stand to take it
Wherever we stand!

Where goes then this road
And what is its end?
Is there here of us these
And of those there, them!

But beauty....beckons.
Moving – Becoming

GOD AND THE DEVIL

I came from the place we know not all well
Then into this life at once my soul fell
So that once within me this life holds a bevel
I will that I live by God and the devil

Though cares and though woes do cast on their spell
And waters dry out from the life's living well
And earth becomes scorched such that all hills be level
I will that I live by God and the devil

So troubles sure come from the places they swell
And rendings and torments direct me to hell
I round up the base, and will echo this treble
I will that I live by God and the devil

The pushes and pulls by which life cares compell
The fright of the turtle reclined in the shell
Are windows in time when I speak to it's rebel
I will that I live by God and the devil

So guide ye and guard ye the paths of the way
And drop ye a breadcrumb at each random stray
For when all is done and the plan moves to play
By God and the devil we live come what may

It just is...like that!

SRB. Times.

BLUE HANDS

Whole hands of fingers touching the keys
That share news of opinionated views
Sharing blurry frames of captured self same
Tags with names
Joy between friends of time- bound ends
The faces seen in places been

Glassy mazes replace faces once we knew
Gentle pings of things beyond the blue
While apples fall into places shared to pixels placed
These dont erase the ease with which we squeeze together
This just to say, another day. To chart our way

Way off from bidding comforts hold
Still to be told how things at end unfold
The journeys hope no more a care
Since we seem always there. Always near...

To the place that thought holds square
In focus
Snaps of thoughts of Psycolocus.

Away to go... elsewhere to show
Up streaming inclined water falls
Touching keys, making the call soft and loud
As blue descends to cloud

BELIEF WITHIN, SELF WITHOUT

Consider that the self exist in the other
Within dwells the locus of our purest beliefs
The locus of mentation
While objectively we ex-ist objectively
In the other!

The heart within left
While it ex-ist to our right
Likewise the East!
Left as belief
Right as ,ex-ist

The mirror instructs
As the water also...
And where is in it the basis of ex- istence?
The waters instruct
The locus of belief
The locus of ex- istence

Right is left
So, what's left?!

Seeds, drives, causes are right
Hearts declare
Now, what's left?

The Oneness, of the thingness of things
Fractally dispersed
Dually experienced
As conscious cause?

The Psycolocus

SRB.11.2024.

BEGINNINGS

Grounded resounds of unknown things
Echo reflections that wave
Together one
Weaved
Flowerings of life's eternal flame
Subtlety
Becometh sight

Once, then again
Their rhythm sway decree
muffled master's misted call
Thingless thought
Becomes all

Fruitful
Though as airy beings
Their life's work now performed
They stand
The substance of the landed hand

True mastered stake!

SRB. 13.2.2025

AVA DENSE

There is magic in the eyes
Giving thought throughout the years

There is magic In the numbers
That amount the sum of cares

There is mystery in beginnings
Of the divers scores and weights

There is ghostly curiosity
In dispensation of our faith

There is so much, of so many
Things that curb and bind and heal

There is such that gives us buoyancy
Much that magnetize our steel

Much considering of the journeys
Pathways narrow, pathways wide

Much debacle some diversions
Surfing waves and stemming tide

Yet of all the much, and many things
That thought and sense combine

Is the mystery of the moment
Tis the mastery of the mind

And through it all and in it all at last appears the best
The proof within the mettle, is its motion, pause and rest!

SRB. 30.11.2024

ALL GOOD THINGS

All good things so together flow
Their beauty is displayed
All good seeds come
Full from the seed
All night becomes a day

Through clouded air
And sifted sun
Through tempered vibrance cast
The toiling of the forrow
Fruits tomorrow
Yield at last

SRB. 12.2025

ABYSMAL ARTISAN

Sometimes our dutiful tireless Sun
Winks at us a smile
We see
In this chance encounter
The tireless artisan
Ceaselessly drawing on all
That dwells
Latent in the abyss

Now casting forth with beauty
Splendour
The majestic universe

Upon a canvas
Of spacetime fabric
On which canvass we ourselves
Having place,
Created the magical piece
With power
To escape
All this becomes
The pinnacle
Of beauty!
A wonderful world this is.

SRB 02.03.2025

ABOVE CHAOS

Cosmic lifelines
Escaped of
By cause

Nomadic

Free floating
Cobs finding safe
Lodgings amidst thorns

The memory
Of these come rue
Bidding wordless thoughts
Ginning thoughtless words

Ends of Cordless
Waves
Afloat.

4 ME

What then?
Does nature hold a lie
Of how her Orbits are to be?

Does not two flow
Together one
Like rivers to the sea?

Does not the thing
That being so made
Encircle all its cares?

And does the balance
Not account
For all that is prepared?

What then?
Think we
As mortal man
Such course to change its speed

When at a bet
We cast at nought
The formal cause of deed

That seeing not

We plant an ive
Of words that are at seed

All forms built in
We spell without
Our point in space to make

So that which comes
Of natures take
Reveals of us our stake

And when the art is finished
Our spheres we cast a spin
Know we not well
That this our work
Became so of our gin?

For energy is motion
It flows so here
Then there

And knowing this
We now can choose
Our words
With utmost care

Disclaimer

The poems in this collection are inspired by real-life experiences; however, they are not intended to reference or reflect any specific individual, event, or circumstance. Any perceived connection to actual persons or situations is purely coincidental. The author affirms that there is no intent to target, harm, or misrepresent any individual or event in any way.

www.ingramcontent.com/pod-product-compliance
Lightning Source LLC
LaVergne TN
LVHW021408080426
835508LV00020B/2498